HEREI
Gho

Prepare to be frightened by these terrifying tales from
around Herefordshire

By

Richard Holland

BRADWELL
BOOKS

Published by Bradwell Books
9 Orgreave Close Sheffield S13 9NP
Email: books@bradwellbooks.co.uk

British Library Cataloguing in Publication Data: a catalogue
record for this book is available from the British Library.
1st Edition

ISBN: 9781909914933

Design & Typesetting by: JenksDesign

Photograph Credits: iStock and R. Holland

Print: Gomer Press, Llandysul, Ceredigion SA44 4JL

CONTENTS

A dramatic painting of Goodrich Castle by the 19th-century artist 'Grecian' Williams. The ruined castle is arguably the most impressive haunted location in Herefordshire.

Hereford has several haunted locations, including its splendid cathedral.
iStock

INTRODUCTION

Herefordshire, on the Welsh Border, was fought over for centuries. This is hardly surprising. It is one of the most beautiful and richly fertile counties in the UK. Well into the Middle Ages Herefordshire was considered part of Wales, and the Welsh didn't give it up easily. Its peaceful countryside and mellow towns and villages give little sense of the turbulent years of those past conflicts.

The only clues to those violent times are the numerous castles dotted throughout the county, many only surviving as decayed but in some cases magnificent ruins. These fortresses also saw action during the equally bloody upheavals of the English Civil War. All this drama has inevitably led to the telling of folk tales by those living in the shadows of these splendid monuments. It is no surprise to find that Herefordshire is considered an especially haunted county.

In this book you will encounter a diverse and fascinating range of spooks, including lords and ladies, monks and nuns, knights and cavaliers, phantom animals and ghosts that are never actually seen. You will read of the battles between troublesome spirits and the clergymen who struggled to subdue them; of ghosts which accost people at night and force them to do their bidding; of headless ghosts and a head without a body; and of the Wild Hunt which rides through the Herefordshire skies at night searching for wicked souls to drag to Hell.

Despite all this spookiness, however, it is worth remembering that Herefordshire was the place where the term 'picturesque' was first coined. If this book inspires you to visit some of the county's haunted places for yourself, you will also be exploring some of England's prettiest countryside.

I hope you enjoy this guide to Herefordshire's haunted heritage.

GHOSTS WITH A PURPOSE

Traditional ghost stories often tell of people being accosted by troubled spirits who have become trapped on the mortal plane. Typically they have committed wrongs in life which they never had the chance to put right, or they have hidden valuables or important documents which need uncovering. Since they are unable to move on to the next world until these needs are satisfied, the ghosts can be exceedingly demanding in forcing people to help them.

Take, for example, the tale of Old Taylor, which dates from the early 19th century. Old Taylor had been the owner of a farm called Morning Pits which in those days stood just outside Hereford. His ghost had taken to wandering around the Whitecross district of the city. Sometimes he would ride about on a spectral pony; on other occasions he would be seen sitting on a stile. How Old Taylor's spirit finally found peace was related in an article in the *Hereford Times*, published in 1876.

'One stormy night,' goes the report, 'a fellow walked into the bar of the Nag's Head [now The Monument pub], and said he had seen Old Taylor, and had promised to meet him in the Morning Pits that night at twelve. Of course nobody believed him, and as the night wore on the others jeered at him and said, "I would not go on such a night as this."

'He said he would not; but as the hour drew near he was obliged to go. Something forced him to run, so that he reached the Morning Pits as the clock struck twelve. There the old man [i.e. Old Taylor] was waiting. "Follow me," said he. The man followed him into some strange place, which they seemed to reach in a very short time. In the place were two immense stones.

"Take up these stones," said Old Taylor. "I can't," says Denis (he was nicknamed Denis the Liar). "You can," said Taylor, "try." He tried, and lifted the stones easily. "Now come with me," said Taylor, "and place them where I shall show you."

'He carried them and put them down with ease. "Now", said Old Taylor, "I caution you never to tell anybody what you saw here this night." Denis promised. "And now," said Old Taylor, "lie down on your face and as you value your life don't attempt to look either way until you hear music, and then get away as fast as you can."

'Denis lay a long time without hearing what he earnestly desired, but at last the welcome sound of music was heard. Denis the Liar was a different man after that, though he soon died from the effects of the night.'

The task Denis the Liar was forced to perform by the ghost bears some explanation. Old Taylor was bound to the earth because he had unlawfully moved a pair of marker stones on the boundary of his estate. In this way he had apparently increased the extent of his own land to the detriment of his neighbour. A number of other ghost stories around the UK relate to landowners returning from the dead for committing this crime, so it may have been perceived as a common problem in the past.

Whatever the reason for a ghost needing a mortal's help, in these stories the person they approach find themselves compelled to do so, never mind how scared they are. And, like Denis the Liar, they may be taken to the necessary location at supernatural speed. After the matter has been dealt with, they are frequently asked to lie face down while the ghost vanishes into the ether. In this tale and the next the mortal man is told to wait until music is heard, although Old Taylor did not specify what sort of music.

Restless spirits have been known to force their way into people's lives, compelling them to carry out a task that will allow them to lie easy in their graves. iStock

This is made clearer in the following story. Another common theme is that those who have been compelled to help a ghost often suffer as a result and, like Denis, soon pass away themselves.

The following three stories all feature farm labourers, two of whom are called Tom, and all are said to have taken place in the 19th century. After sundown, Tom, a labourer at Devereux Wootton Farm, south of Weobley, kept meeting a mysterious woman on his way home to Kinnersley. He realised she was not of this world, and would hurry past her, ignoring the pleading look in her eyes. One night, however, he found the ghost sitting on a stile, blocking his way. He had no choice but to ask her to move.

'I have waited for years for someone to speak to me,' she said. Now she was free to act as she liked, and she compelled poor Tom to accompany her back to Devereux Wootton Farm. When they arrived, Tom was amazed to see that the farmhouse was illuminated as if every lamp in the place had been lit. Not only that, but the doors were wide open. Everyone inside was fast asleep, however. The unearthly woman, who told Tom that she was the spirt of a certain Lady Berrington, was clearly familiar with the place, for she strode through a number of rooms until she came to an old oak chest. This opened to her touch and she removed a roll of documents. These she handed to Tom, instructing him to throw them into the middle of a nearby pool.

Shooed out of the house by Lady Berrington's ghost, Tom did as she had commanded, taking care not to look at any of the writing on the documents. The spirit had warned him of the dire consequences that would befall him if he did so. She also told him that as soon as the paper slipped below the surface of the water, he would hear either beautiful music or horrible voices. If he heard the music, it meant he was destined for Heaven when he died, but the alternative meant he was bound for Hell. Fortunately, he heard the heavenly music but alas he broke another of Lady Berrington's taboos. She ordered him never to tell anyone what had happened, but he couldn't resist gossiping about it. The result was that he sickened and 'he was never right afterwards'.

From Craswall comes another story of this type. A labourer was sitting by his meagre fire one night in his room at Black Hill Farm, when he was startled to see a deathly white face peering in at his window. 'Who's there?' he called out but the stranger made no reply. Whoever it was apparently stepped back into the darkness and vanished from view. The labourer rushed outside

*An amusing old illustration of an autocratic ghost and the frightened man
it has brought to a secret hiding place.*

but there was no sign of anyone. The same thing happened again, and then the next night. Realising it must be a ghost, the labourer commanded the spirit in the name of God to tell him how he could help it. It's an ancient tradition that a spirit cannot interact with a mortal until a holy name is uttered.

This spirit wasted no time with explanations, however; it simply grabbed hold of the hapless labourer and dragged him out into the cold night air. He found himself propelled through the countryside at supernatural speed until he was brought to a sudden stop by a dry stone wall. At last the spirit spoke. It ordered its unwilling companion to remove a number of stones in the wall, which he did. Behind them he found a box, which he was ordered to pick up. No sooner was it in his hands, than he was again whisked away through the air. At last they came to the banks of a pool, and into this the labourer was told to throw the box. Once it had sunk from sight, the ghost vanished. The weary, frightened man was left to find his own way home. The entire ordeal proved too much for him. He never enjoyed good health again and died an early death.

Another farm labourer, Tom Reece, is the hero in the final story of this type. In contrast to the previous accounts, the troubled soul encountered by Tom was known to him, although this wasn't immediately apparent.

Tom was walking home to Hoarwithy from a night out in Ross-on-Wye when he got the eerie feeling he was being followed. He looked behind him and saw that a huge, black hound was approaching him down the moonlit lane. It was a fearsome-looking beast and Tom was worried it might attack him. Rather than risk having it chase him, Tom decided it would be safer not to quicken his pace but to calmly step aside and let the hound pass him on the lane. He did so, but the animal behaved like no ordinary dog. It sat down and regarded him with an almost human intelligence. After they had stared at each other for a few, long moments, Tom reluctantly continued his journey. Immediately, the hound began to follow him again, staying the same distance apart, literally dogging his footsteps.

The pad-pad-pad of the huge hound behind him understandably soon got on Tom's nerves. He turned and shouted at it to be off, but again it just sat down in the lane until Tom turned round and continued his walk. More frustrated now than frightened, Tom yanked a stick out of the hedgerow and lobbed it at the hound. The stick bounced off its head but the dog didn't even flinch. Tom rummaged in the hedge until he found a really big stick. Wielding it in one hand, uttering all sorts of threats, Tom advanced on the dog, hoping to drive it away without having to resort to further violence. But now something really weird happened. As soon as Tom got within a couple of yards of it, the dog suddenly stood up – on two legs!

Tom jumped back and looked on aghast as the dog changed before his eyes, transforming itself into the shape of a human being. It was somebody he had known very well: it was his dead father. Terror now gripping his heart, Tom waited to see no more. He ran blindly down the lane, as fast as he could, until he eventually reached his home in a state of exhaustion. Poor Tom was in shock for some days. His family noticed that he was troubled and depressed but he could not bring himself to tell them what he had seen.

One night, things came to a head. Tom's brother awoke to find him, fully dressed, creeping out of the room. Tom hushed him back to sleep, telling him that he would be back soon and not to worry. There is a gap in the story here, for when we next hear of Tom he is at a nearby wood, where he finds the mysterious black dog waiting for him. It is a fair guess that prior to this particular evening he has been accosted by the spirit of his father in the same way that Denis was accosted by Old Taylor, for how else would he know where to meet the ghost?

The dog crept into the wood and Tom followed it into the shadow of the trees. It was hard to follow the black dog through the gloom, twisting its way between the tree trunks, but after a while the animal came to a halt in a clearing. It turned to face Tom and then transformed itself back into the spectre of his father. The ghost pointed to the ground beside it and uttered just one word, in a commanding voice: 'Dig!'

The story does not explain how Tom was able to comply with this command – he may have been forewarned and had armed himself with a shovel – but dig he did, in the spot indicated by the shade of his father. Soon he had uncovered a leather satchel, hidden in the damp earth. He hauled it out. The ghost spoke again: 'Throw it in the river.' Tom and his father's spirit headed to the nearest stretch of the River Wye and there, with a determined heave, the young man hurled the bag into the water. He had not dared to see what was inside it and never found out. Apparently satisfied, the ghost of Tom's father vanished. Such had been the strain that Tom passed out, but when he was awakened by the dawn, he was a new man, no longer oppressed in spirit. He was never troubled by ghosts again.

Tom was lucky in that his encounter with a needy ghost had no lasting effects on his health. You will have noticed that in three of these stories the hidden valuables are recovered only to be sunk out of sight again within the waters of a pool or river. This is a common theme in stories of this type and may reflect a folk memory of the offerings made to bodies of water by our Celtic ancestors. Many of the finest artefacts recovered from the Iron

Age have been found in lakes, marshes and rivers, deposited as a form of sacrifice.

Spectral black dogs are also a feature of British ghost-lore. Similar ghosts are claimed for almost every English county, with many other examples in Wales and Scotland, too. Elsewhere, they go by various names, such as Padfoot in Yorkshire, Skryker in Lancashire, Black Shuck in East Anglia, Gwyllgi ('Dog of the Twilight') in Wales and Cu Sith ('Fairy Dog') in Scotland. They all have similarities, such as being huge in size, more or less canine in appearance, often with shaggy coats, and with unearthly features such as being headless or possessing glowing red eyes. They also share the common characteristic of following benighted travellers along lonely roads and paths.

Some think the belief in them dates back to the Anglo-Saxon period because the god Woden was said to be accompanied by a monstrous black hound. The mysterious, still uncatchable black panthers supposed to roam wild places like Dartmoor and Bodmin Moor may merely be a modern interpretation of these enigmatic apparitions. We will encounter more spectral black dogs in subsequent chapters.

Sherlock Holmes and Dr Watson catch sight of the Hound of the Baskervilles in Conan Doyle's famous story. This fictional hound was inspired by legends of spectral black dogs such as those encountered in Herefordshire. Some say the Black Hound of Hergest in the following chapter was the model Doyle drew on when he came up with the Baskerville legend.

BLACK VAUGHAN AND OTHER EXORCISMS

Ghosts could not only be troublesome but also hard to get rid of and many traditional tales relate the struggles of clergymen attempting to do so. Exorcism was a word largely unknown to our rural ancestors, who would more usually refer to the practice as 'ghost-laying'. The phrase 'to pray down' a ghost was also used, for the process involved firstly taming the ghost and then slowly reducing it in size to something small and manageable, such as a fly or a spider. In this form, the spirit could be trapped in a box or a bottle and disposed of.

The trapped spirits were usually deposited in bodies of water, as suggested by a biblical reference to the Red Sea. Particularly favoured was the water beneath bridges. Bridges have a special significance in traditional ghost-lore because they are 'between places'. Stiles and crossroads were perceived as having the same otherworldly significance. Sometimes a so-called 'ban' was put upon the spirit, a bargain to keep it imprisoned for a specific number of years. The ghost-laying may only have been a temporary measure.

Black Vaughan was one such ghost which required subduing. Thomas Vaughan ap Rosser was born in 1400 and earned the name Black Vaughan either because of his dark hair and swarthy complexion or perhaps because of his dark deeds. Vaughan was the lord of Hergest Court, a splendid medieval mansion near Kington whose gardens are now open to the public. During the War of the Roses Vaughan sided with the House of York and was captured and beheaded by Lancastrians. His body was returned to Herefordshire, however, and interred in Kington Church, along with his wife, beneath a beautiful marble sculpture of the pair of them lying side by side.

Black Vaughan's spirit did not lie easy in its elegant grave, however. It became a terror to the neighbourhood. Sometimes it would take the form of a bull and would charge roaring into the church, interrupting the sermon and scattering the congregation. In the form of a huge fly, it would torment horses to madness. His ghost would also lurk around a particular oak tree; although invisible, his presence was given away by two scorch marks in the grass where his feet were standing. The ghost was so strong that it could overturn farmers' wagons in the lanes. Some people claimed to see Vaughan's head floating around above the moat of Hergest Court, in a bizarre reversal of the usual headless ghost theme.

Such a state of affairs could not be allowed to continue and the people of Kington begged the clergy to do something to lay Black Vaughan's malevolent spirit. The story of what happened was passed down the generations and was still current into the 20th century. The well-known Victorian diarist Francis Kilvert, curate and then vicar at a number of churches either side of the Herefordshire–Radnorshire border, learnt one version of the adventure from a mole-catcher. Kilvert noted it down in his diary:

'Twelve or thirteen ancient parsons assembled in the court of Hergest and drew a circle, inside which they all stood with books and lighted candles, praying. The ghost was very resolute and came among the parsons roaring like a bull. "Why so fierce, Mr Vaughan?" asked one of the parsons mildly. "Fierce I was as a man, fiercer still as a devil!" roared Vaughan, and all the candles were blown out except one, held by a very small, weak parson. He hid the candle in his boots and so kept it alight, all the time praying hard until at length the violent spirit was quelled, and brought down so small and humble that they shut him up in a

Two views of Hergest Court, where the ghost of Black Vaughan made such a nuisance of itself.

snuff box. The ghost made one humble petition – "Do not bury me beneath water." But the parson immediately had him enclosed in a stone box, and buried him under the bed of the brook and Hergest was henceforth at peace.'

In the version told to Ella Mary Leather, author of *The Folk-Lore of Herefordshire*, published in 1912, a woman and a newborn baby joined the parsons, presumably as symbols of purity. Vaughan's ghost begged specifically not to be banished to the Red Sea and instead the box in which he had been trapped was sunk in the deepest part of a pool close by Hergest Court, and a heavy stone placed on top of it. The period for which Vaughan was compelled to remain in this watery prison was not specified to Mrs Leather but her informant warned her: 'The time is nearly up!'

In 1940 there was distress in the neighbourhood when it was learnt that the then owner of Hergest Court planned to drain the pool and, worse still, had discovered a big stone within it, which he intended to raise. Rumours abounded that the apparition of Black Vaughan was still to be seen near the pool and the owner changed his mind when, as the work began to drain it away, the water 'began to bubble ominously'. He quickly had the pool shored up again. Roy Palmer, author of *Herefordshire Folklore*, published in 2002, was told of this incident by the late owner's daughter.

In addition to Black Vaughan's ghost, Hergest Court was said to be haunted by his pet dog, a huge, black hound. The hound manifested whenever one of Vaughan's descendants was due to die, roaming through the house, dragging after it a monstrous clanking chain. Some believe the Black Hound of Hergest Court was the inspiration for Arthur Conan Doyle's Sherlock Holmes story *The Hound of the Baskervilles*.

An exorcism very similar to the one described above is also related about Hereford Cathedral. Here the ghost was a benign one, the spirit of a member of the cathedral staff called Hoskins, who died in 1786. Although he caused no one any harm, the cathedral clergy decided that it was unseemly to have a ghost wandering around their place of worship and they set about exorcising it. Twelve clergymen assembled just before midnight, each bearing a lighted candle. As the cathedral bells tolled twelve times, they summoned the ghost to appear before them. At last, it was compelled to do so but the formerly placid spirit of Mr Hoskins now became aggressive. Like the ghost of Black Vaughan, it is said to have yelled at the exorcists something to the effect of, 'Fierce I was as a man, fiercer still now I am a devil!'

The outraged spook did everything in its power to prevent the exorcism going ahead. It blew out the candles one by one and caused a terrible commotion in the cathedral, shaking its ancient stone walls like an earthquake. Eventually, only one candle was left alight, that belonging to a Canon Underwood. Elderly and frail though he was, Canon Underwood succeeded in subduing Mr Hoskins's ghost, which had tired itself out by this time, and he shrunk it down so small that he was able to trap it in a bottle. This was buried under a bridge at Byster's Gate in the city. The battle with the ghost had put so much strain on the cathedral, however, that shortly afterwards the West Tower collapsed. (More tales of Hereford Cathedral follow in the next chapter.)

In 1921, folklorist Andrew Haggard overheard two old men discussing the laying of a ghost which had occurred when they were children. The ghost on this occasion was the first wife of the blacksmith in the village of Acton Cross. She was an even gentler spirit than Mr Hoskins at Hereford Cathedral, for her sole reason for returning from the dead was to protect her children from the cruelty of their stepmother. Here is the story as told to Mr

Medieval clergymen seek to exorcise a demon interfering with the building of their church.

Haggard and repeated in his book *Dialect and Local Usages of Herefordshire*. I've edited it of unnecessary digression, but have retained the local dialect, with its peculiar spellings:

'Mrs Hodges dies and leaves two children, and the blacksmith he marries again, and very quick he did too and her was bad to the children of the first wife. And the first wife's sperrit took to haanting her children, not terrifying them as you might say, but just standing at their beds. And the children they warn't frightened neither, cos she had her clothes on [her ordinary clothes, that is, rather than the shroud she would have been buried in].

'But her come that strong that all the place was talking on it. And they tells the parson and he lays un and says – parson says he don't never want no such job again – fair made him sweat, it did. Copeland were parson then. And he got eleven other parsons so there was twelve on 'em, each with a lit candle, and they start to read her small [i.e. prayed her down to a more manageable size]. Least they raised un first 'cos with sperrits you got to raise un afore you falls un. And her come that big and the lights went out and at last there was only one candle left, and fortunate that candle kept burning else she'd 'a bested them. And they got reading her smaller and smaller and got her real small and pushed un in a matchbox and thrown un in Amstell Pond and her aren't troubled no one since.'

It seems a shame that this watchful mother should have been disposed of in this way, for one can't help wondering about the welfare of her children once their stepmother had no more reason to fear ghostly retribution.

It is apparent from all these tales that to keep a light burning when dealing with angry spirits is essential. This motif also appears in a story of an exorcism related to Avenbury Church, near Bromyard. St Mary's in Avenbury was abandoned in the 1930s and has since been deconsecrated. It is now a creepy, crumbling ruin among a tangle of trees and undergrowth.

Even today the church has a sinister reputation, with rumours of Satanic rituals taking place in it after dark. A procession of phantom monks has been seen among the trees, and witnesses have related hearing a bell tolling in its empty tower and of organ music echoing from its crumbling walls. The spooky music was heard even before the church became a ruin. The organ was frequently heard playing when the church was locked and presumed empty. Andrew Haggard, mentioned above, spoke to a man who had heard the music himself. He related to Mr Haggard the legend behind the haunting. It involved two brothers who came to blows:

'The one, he were a good chap and 'a used to play the organ in the church reg'lar,' he said. 'Everybody liked un. T'other he were a sclem [good-for-nothing], never did no work and was allus a-pothering his brother for money and such. Nobody couldn't suffer un. How it come to happen I don't rightly know, but one evening they comes to blows on the water bridge over the prill

An exorcism being carried out in the early 19th century. The ghost or possessed man is crawling down the stairs, at the right. Note the man on the left holding a candle.

[brook] just off the Bromyard road, and the one he kills his brother for dead. And that weren't the end of it, not by no manner of means, for arter that the organ used to play nights, and no lights nor nobody there. A could hear un on the road and all quiet – there's scores heered un one time or another.'

In the hope of silencing the ghostly music, the vicar of St Mary's decided to visit the little bridge where the murder had been committed and so lay the restless spirit of the murdered man. He armed himself with candles but in the struggle of wills with the spirit, two out of the three he had lit were blown out. However, this one flared up brighter than all three put together and this signalled the successful end to the exorcism. The organ music has continued to be heard from time to time but it is less strident than before, or, to put it in the words of Mr Haggard's informant: 'The pain had gone out of it.'

A unique but apparently successful attempt at quietening a ghost was long ago reported from Bronsil Castle, a fortified manor house near Eastnor. During the English Civil War, the Roundheads captured the castle and then set fire to it to ensure it couldn't be used again by the Royalists. The gatehouse survived more or less intact for many years but it too partially collapsed in the 1990s. The ghost haunting the remains of Bronsil Castle is a knight in armour, and so pre-dates the Civil War by several centuries.

The knight's haunting began for some unknown reason in 1605 when Bronsil Castle was the home of the Reede family. The local ghost-layer told the head of the house, Gabriel Reede, that the phantom was probably a defunct member of the family who had originally built Bronsil back in the 13th century, the Beauchamps. He told him that the best way to quieten the ghost would be to collect together some bones of one of the defunct

Beauchamps and bring them to Bronsil. Reede broke open the tomb of Lord John Beauchamp, and removed several vertebrae from the skeleton which had lain there undisturbed since 1475. These he put in a box, wrote 'Lord Beauchamp's Bones' on it, and then secreted it away in Bronsil Castle. This peculiar remedy worked and the phantom knight ceased his nocturnal perambulations.

Decades later, when the Roundheads attacked Bronsil Castle, the garrison fled, and took Lord Beauchamp's bones away with them. They remained at New Court, the Reedes' second residence, for more than 200 years. However, they were lost (or thrown out) sometime in the 19th century and the unknown knight immediately began haunting Bronsil Castle again, apparently unaware that it is no longer patrolling rooms and

The ruin of Bronsil Castle, drawn in the 19th century at about the time the ghostly knight began to haunt it again.

corridors, but only patches of broken masonry and grass and weeds.

More stories of ghosts haunting ruined castles can be found in the final chapter.

ARTHUR, EDRIC AND OTHER HEROES

There are a number of ancient kings and noblemen who feature in Herefordshire ghost-lore. They are otherworldly, larger-than-life characters, and more than one are linked to an old and rather frightening phenomenon known as the Wild Hunt. One of these is the legendary King Arthur.

King Arthur has been claimed for various parts of the British Isles, but Wales arguably has the best claim, at least in terms of the earliest sources referring to him. If so, it would be reasonable to suppose that he spent some time in Herefordshire, and there are a number of traditions to support this. Arthur's Stone is a Stone Age burial chamber on Merbach Hill above Dorstone. Here it was said King Arthur fought and won a duel with a rival warrior, and the monument was named after him from then on. A King Arthur's Cave can be found in The Doward, a hill near Symonds Yat.

King Arthur's ghost has been seen near Hoarwithy, riding along beside a stretch of the River Wye called the Red Rail. He is in the company of a number of other knights, apparently all riding out for a day's hunting.

King Arthur's legendary wizard, Merlin, also has connections with Herefordshire. There is a Merlin's Cave, for example, close to King Arthur's Cave. His weird figure, dressed in rags, is said to haunt Longtown Castle, a Norman fortification now in ruins and managed by English Heritage. In his book *Haunted Herefordshire*, author Rupert Matthews suggests that this is the apparition of a real Welsh poet, active in the 6th century, called Merddyn Wyllt. Merddyn supposedly went mad after seeing his countrymen defeated in a bloody battle and took to wandering the countryside, much as the legendary Merlin was said to have done. According to Mr Matthews, Merddyn Wyllt was buried close to where the castle ruins now stand.

Another legendary character based on a real man is 'Wild Edric', thought to have been Edric Salvage, who is recorded in the Domesday Book of 1086 as an Anglo-Saxon nobleman with extensive estates in Herefordshire and Shropshire. Edric resisted the Norman Conquest for a number of years but soon saw which side his bread was best buttered on and made peace with William I. Some years later, however, he attempted to throw off the Norman yoke again and his estates were forfeited. After that he seems to have become something of a guerrilla leader but his eventual fate is not known.

A fascinating story about him was set down in the 12th century by historian and clergyman Walter Map. Map, who was in the running to become Bishop of Hereford in 1199, had family at Wormsley and is known to have owned land at Ullingswick. Educated at the University of Paris and a popular courtier to King Henry II, Map is thought to have written a great deal of work both historical and literary, including a cycle of satirical poems and, possibly, a version of the legend of Sir Lancelot, King Arthur's right-hand man. Unfortunately, only one work survives, a gossipy collection of legends and anecdotes called *De*

Nugis Curialium ('Trifles of Courtiers'), which was first published in about the year 1180. The 'Trifles', however, contain much of interest to folklorists and reveal that even educated men of the Middle Ages were willing to believe in a great deal of what today we would consider fantastical.

The ruins of Longtown Castle, where you may see the ghost of the wizard Merlin.

Map's story of Wild Edric sees him becoming lost in a vast forest on the Welsh Borders while out hunting. After wandering around for hours, he saw a light shining through the trees. He made his way towards it and came across a building in the depths of the woods. Peering through a window, he watched in wonder as a number of beautiful, stately women danced in a circle. One in particular attracted him. He burst his way in, grabbed the girl who had taken his fancy and carried her away before anyone could stop him.

Somehow Edric found his way back to his court, his captive in tow. The woman's beauty captivated everyone, but she refused to speak for three days and nights. Then she relented and told Edric she was prepared to marry him, on the condition that he allowed her to return to the forest to meet her sisters when she felt like it and that he should never reproach her for doing so. If he broke this promise, she warned him, she would instantly leave him and calamity would come upon him. Edric agreed and he and the lovely woman from the woods were married. For many years they lived in harmony together and Edric showed no jealousy over his wife's regular visits to her sisters. One fateful day, however, he returned from hunting to find the house empty. By the time his wife eventually returned, Edric was in a foul temper.

'I suppose it was those sisters of yours who kept you so long?' he growled. That was enough. The injunction had been broken. His wife vanished in the wink of an eye and though he searched and searched, Edric found neither his wife nor the mysterious building in the woods again. He became ill and listless, he lost his home and his estates and died of despair.

This rather tragic yarn is a version of a widely told folk tale regarding men who succeed in abducting fairy brides. The 'fairies' who feature in other stories of this type from the same period are clearly identified as being spirits of the dead, however. In another account very similar to that of Wild Edric, a nobleman who spies women dancing in a wood recognises one of them as his own wife, who had passed away the previous year.

On the Welsh Borders 'Wild Edric' became something of a folk hero, in the King Arthur mould. One legend had it that he and his wife and all his court remain sleeping underground, waiting for England to be restored to a time resembling the nation he knew, before the Norman Conquest. In neighbouring

A Victorian representation of the Wild Hunt, a phenomenon represented in Herefordshire by Wild Edric and King Herla. iStock

Shropshire, lead miners would claim to hear him knocking on the walls of the passages underground to indicate where rich seams of ore could be found.

In Herefordshire Edric has passed into legend as a ghost. He is said to be seen riding around his former estates at Burrington, in company of a fierce band of soldiers. Edric wears magnificent armour and he and his men are all fully armed. There are also stories of Edric and his war band galloping through the night sky, their bloodthirsty whoops and yells emanating from the clouds, terrifying anyone below who happens to hear them. Here they are taking the place of the Wild Hunt, an Anglo-Saxon and Norse superstition in which the god Woden or Odin rode out to hunt down the souls of the wicked.

The apparition mentioned above of King Arthur and his men riding as if engaged in a hunt may also have once been regarded as an example of the Wild Hunt. A more definite link is again made by Walter Map to another ancient notable, King Herla, semi-legendary King of the Britons (i.e. the Welsh). In Map's story, Herla was making preparations for his wedding when a 'pygmy' arrived at his court, riding on a goat. The pygmy paid his compliments to the king and asked leave to attend the wedding. Herla courteously issued him with an invitation.

A year later, the king was a guest at the pygmy's own wedding, in a palace carved out of solid rock, accessed through a cave near Bunshill. Here Herla, his queen and numerous courtiers were lavishly entertained but – alas! – without realising it, they had been all this time in fairyland, where time runs differently to the world of mortals. Centuries had gone by while they had enjoyed what appeared to them to be a mere three days of celebrations. When two of Herla's knights dismounted from their horses and touched the earth, they crumbled into dust. The king and queen and the rest of the retinue were doomed to ride through the land for evermore, ghost-like, unable to fully rejoin the mortal world. In time they became the Wild Hunt. Phantom horsemen are said to still be seen in the vicinity of Bunshill.

Linked to the Wild Hunt are the Cŵn Annwn, whose name in Welsh means 'Dogs of the Underworld'. A number of Welsh superstitions have lingered in Herefordshire, for it too was part of Wales at one time. Unlike the solitary black dogs of the type we have previously encountered at Hergest Court and Craswall, the Cŵn Annwn always haunted in packs. I might as fairly have written 'hunted' as 'haunted', for, like the Wild Hunt, their prey was sinful souls. Woe betide any individual out after dark who encountered them, for unless they were absolutely without sin, they risked being dragged away by the Cŵn Annwn back to Hell.

Some stories of the Cŵn Annwn, or their equivalents in England, state that the Devil himself was the master of these hounds. Tradition has it that the baying of the Cŵn Annwn could once upon a time be heard in the air above Paton's Cross, at Eardisley. Many years ago, the manor house at Eardisley was owned by the Baskerville family, providing another possible connection with Conan Doyle's *Hound of the Baskervilles*.

More recent than the previous noblemen and women is the Welsh freedom fighter Owain Glyndŵr (Shakespeare's Owen Glendower). Owain staged a revolt against King Henry IV after a dispute over land near Ruthin in Denbighshire. He had previously been a loyal supporter of Henry and may even have acted as his squire at one time. He had also served as a soldier, fighting the Scots and others, under Richard II. But Henry sided with a Norman baron, Reginald de Grey, against Owain, who felt betrayed.

The Cŵn Annwn hunted in packs in search of sinners. In this splendid illustration by the Victorian artist Brock, they are seen being urged on by the Devil himself.

Initially, Owain's uprising proved successful and he was able to expel the English from a number of territories in Wales. He was crowned Prince of Wales and teamed up with two disgruntled English lords in the hope of carving up England and Wales between them. Within a decade, the rebellion was quashed, however, and Owain Glyndŵr had become a hunted man, continuing a form of guerrilla warfare until he disappeared from history in 1412. He was never captured and no one knows what became of him.

One possibility is that Owain divided his time between three Herefordshire houses owned by the husbands of his daughters: Croft Castle, Kentchurch Court and Monnington Court. The first two properties are open to the public, which is handy because it is they which are said to be haunted by the ghost of the Welsh rebel. Croft Castle, at Yarpole, started life as a fortress, but after this was wrecked in the 17th century during the English Civil War, it was rebuilt as a manor house. It is now in the care of the National Trust. It is also said to be haunted by Sir James Croft, who rebuilt the castle. Sir James only appears when building work is being carried out, as if making sure that the old place is still in good repair.

Kentchurch is a medieval manor house in the Monnow Valley and boasts splendid gardens. There was an even older house on the site originally and the Scudamore family has been resident here for more than a thousand years. The house and grounds are open to the public on certain days of the year. Owain Glyndŵr is believed to haunt one of the bedrooms.

Owain Glyndŵr has been linked with another of Herefordshire's legendary characters, Jack of Kent, or Jackie Kent. This individual has been variously written about as a good-hearted rogue of the Robin Hood type and as a wizard who had sold his soul to the Devil but who always got the better of the Evil One thanks to his quick wits. He certainly seems to have taken his name from Kentchurch and it has been suggested that the stories may be exaggerated accounts of the deeds of a real person, living the life of an outlaw. With Glyndŵr's own connection with the house, it is not unreasonable to suppose that this may have been a disguise adopted by the deposed Welsh prince. In addition to Glyndŵr's ghost, the pale face of a young woman seen peering out of one of the windows is said to be the apparition of his daughter, anxiously looking out for him.

Croft Castle at Yarpole is one of three old houses in Herefordshire linked to the Welsh hero Owain Glyndŵr, and his ghost is said to haunt the property. iStock

HAUNTED HEREFORD

As late as the 12th century, Hereford was described as 'in Wales'. This handsome old cathedral city was much fought over in the early Middle Ages. Its name is thought to come from the Anglo-Saxon for 'Ford of the Army', suggesting that soldiers were either based here or were a familiar sight crossing over the River Wye to fight various skirmishes with the Welsh. The city even has a Welsh name, Henffordd, or 'Old Road', referring to a nearby Roman road. It is no surprise to learn that such a historic city has a number of haunted properties. Of these, the most impressive is certainly its cathedral.

Like the city, Hereford Cathedral has had a turbulent history. The site dates back to the Anglo-Saxon period, when a small wooden church was built. This housed the tomb of the Saxon King Ethelbert, who was unlawfully killed by Offa, King of Mercia. Miracles were claimed to have occurred for those praying at the tomb and Ethelbert was canonised. In the 9th century a penitent Mercian nobleman rebuilt the church in stone and it became a cathedral, dedicated to St Ethelbert and St Mary the Virgin. Unfortunately, this building was soon destroyed in a raid by Welsh and Irish or Mercian soldiers (accounts vary). It was replaced by a Norman cathedral, which was enlarged and altered over a great many years. Most of what we see today dates from the 14th to the 16th centuries. During the English Civil War it was used as a temporary fortress and underwent a siege.

There are several strange tales about Hereford Cathedral. In the 12th century the Cathedral Close was allegedly haunted by a walking corpse. After dark it would emerge from the graveyard and prowl around the Close, seeking to approach those who lived there. Like the vampires of Eastern Europe, it brought with it a plague. The inhabitants of the Close shuddered behind their locked doors, terrified lest it should visit them. Anyone who heard it whispering their name through the crack in the door would inevitably sicken and die within a few days.

Finally, it approached the door of a knight, Sir William Laudun, who was lodging in the Close. A brave warrior, he refused to be intimidated by the foul thing and when he heard it whispering his name, he jumped up, threw open the door and promptly beheaded it with his sword. This successfully destroyed the monster and its power. It never walked again and no one else fell ill from the disease it had brought with it.

Another eerie visitor appeared in the following century, according to *The Chronicle* of the medieval historian Bartholomew de Cotton. In 1290 de Cotton noted:

'An unheard of and almost impossible marvel occurred in the Cathedral Church of the Hereford Canons. There a demon in the robes of a canon sat in a stall after matins had been sung. A canon came up to him and asked his reason for sitting there, thinking that the demon was a brother canon. The latter refused to answer and said nothing. The canon was terrified, but believing the demon to be an evil spirit put his trust in the Lord and bade him in the name of Christ and St Thomas de Cantilupe not to stir from that place. For a short time he bravely awaited speech. Receiving no answer he at last went for help. He beat the demon and put him in fetters. He now lies in the prison of the aforesaid St Thomas de Cantilupe.'

It's hard to know what to make of this brief account. Was the mysterious canon really a demon? One might think it was a ghost were it not for the fact that it was physically overpowered and thrown into a prison. Perhaps it was simply some poor soul,

Hereford Cathedral has had an exciting history and many strange tales have been told about this splendid building over the years. iStock

mentally ill and robbed of the power of coherent speech, who was cruelly treated by the superstitious monks. The 'St Thomas de Cantilupe' referred to is a former bishop who was canonised after his death in the 1280s, despite having been excommunicated by the Archbishop of Canterbury after a row (the Pope overturned the excommunication).

In 1055 Hereford Cathedral suffered an attack by an army of Welshmen in retaliation for Edward the Confessor taking some of their land to create the earldom of Hereford. The local regiments were swamped by the invaders, and those few who survived limped back to safety in Hereford, only to find most of the townsfolk fleeing to Worcester. Seven canons stayed behind in the cathedral in the hope of preventing any looting or damage. However, when the bloodthirsty soldiers arrived they did not behave like Christians. The canons met the invaders outside the cathedral and explained that it was a house of God where violence was not welcome. Their entreaties were to no avail: one of the Welshmen slashed at a canon with his sword and the rest immediately followed suit, hacking furiously at the holy men.

One of the canons turned and fled back into the cathedral, making for the high altar, where he hoped to offer up a prayer for salvation. The invaders were close on his heels, however. The monk snatched up the altar cross and held it above his head in the hope that its presence would bring the soldiers to their senses. But it was in vain. He too was slaughtered. The ghost of this unfortunate canon is now said to be seen, a tall figure in white, drifting around the Lady Chapel. The Lady Chapel is thought to be situated where the high altar of the earlier church once stood.

An engraving of Hereford Cathedral as it appeared in the 17th century. The West Tower, to the right, collapsed on Easter Monday, 1786, taking much of the West Front and the spire on the East Tower with it. The disaster has been linked to a violent exorcism which took place in the cathedral not long before.

Today there are rumours that the organ in the cathedral plays itself, like the one which formerly stood in Avenbury Church, mentioned in an earlier chapter. It is supposedly being played by the ghost of one John Bull, an organist from the early 17th century, who cannot resist giving ghostly recitals despite having been in his grave for the best part of 400 years.

We have already met with the ghost of old Mr Hoskins, whose exorcism was so violent that it was the alleged cause of the collapse of Hereford Cathedral's West Tower and frontage (see the 'Black Vaughan and Other Exorcisms' chapter). You may recall that his spirit was consigned to a watery prison beneath a bridge at Byster's Gate. It's possible that Hoskins is now free to roam around, if not in the cathedral, at least in the place he was banished to. People passing this way after dark say they have encountered the shadowy form of an old man, dressed in black. He started being seen after the old gate was demolished, the act of which was thought to have freed him.

St Peter's Church, one of the oldest in Hereford, was founded shortly after the Conquest by a Norman baron, Walter de Lacy. Unfortunately, he failed to see it completed, for as he climbed the church tower during its construction, he slipped on ice and fell to his death. It is not he who haunts the church, however, but a shadowy figure of a monk, its head obscured by a black cowl. The spook was spotted by two policemen on the beat late one night in the 1920s. It was creeping up to the church door and they mistook it for a burglar. They hurried to intercept it, but were startled when the hooded figure vanished through the locked door.

High Town is the name given to Hereford's historic city centre and main shopping area. When the square was being redeveloped in the 1960s, a timber-framed house dating from the 17th century was deemed to be in the way, but rather than being demolished, it was painstakingly moved foot by foot to another position. It now stands, looking rather uncomfortably squeezed, since it is such a narrow building, between two modern shops. In the 19th century the house belonged to an apothecary who continued to haunt the premises after his death. He made a fatal mistake with a prescription and accidentally poisoned his apprentice, who was suffering from toothache. The tragedy sent

The Lady Chapel in Hereford Cathedral, where the white-clad apparition of a murdered monk has been seen.

the chemist into a deep depression from which he never really recovered. His ghost was heard pacing the property for many years, but the unorthodox house move in the 1960s seems to have silenced him.

The most striking building in High Town is the aptly named Old House, built in 1621. It was one of a row of timber-framed houses and shops called Butcher's Row, but by the end of the 19th century this was the only one left standing. It is now a museum, its interior restored to its 17th-century splendour. Staff in the museum have reported a feeling of unease in the upper storeys of Old House, particularly in one of the bedrooms, where the curtains on a four-poster bed have been found pulled closed overnight as if someone had been sleeping there. By contrast, a bed in another room was on one occasion found unmade, the sheets kicked about by someone unknown.

According to David Phelps, author of *Haunted Hereford*, the 16th-century Black Lion pub in Bridge Street is 'the most haunted building in Hereford'. Numerous ghost-hunting groups have visited the old coaching inn, drawn to the Painted Room, named for the murals on its walls. This eerie room is notorious for the sounds of footsteps and other noises heard within it and coming from it. Two apparitions have been reported from the pub. One is of a man wearing a green suit and a hat. He has the unnerving habit of tapping people on the shoulder. The other ghost is of a small girl whom the staff have nicknamed Alice. At one time, it is believed, the Black Lion served as an orphanage and it is assumed that this harmless little spirit dates from that time.

There are a number of other haunted pubs in Hereford. The Queen's Arms, on the corner where Broad Street meets West Street, was built during the Georgian period but its ghost dates from a much earlier age. He is a Saxon, possibly one of those killed when Hereford was attacked in in the early 11th century. Way back then the area where the Queen's Head now stands would have been the on city limits and the defenders would have sought to fight back the invaders from here.

The Orange Tree in King Street also stands on a very old site. Nearby there was a convent, whose graveyard extended over the land where the pub now stands. It is haunted by the sad spectre of a nun. Like so many ghostly nuns, she is believed to have had had an affair with a monk. She fell pregnant by him, which meant that it was no longer possible to hide the illicit relationship.

Her lover was punished by his brothers and she never saw him again. When the child was born, it was immediately taken away from the nun and placed in an orphanage. The heartbroken woman lived out her days behind four grey walls, grieving for her lost lover and her baby, suffering the endless contempt of the other nuns.

The invisible ghost of the Horse & Groom in Eign Street has a very different personality: its favourite trick is to pat women on their bottoms. The spook in the Lichfield Vaults, Church Street, enjoys throwing beer mats about and shifting around the beer barrels in the cellar. The Oxford Arms in Widemarsh Street is haunted by a girl who died in a fire centuries ago when the building was used as a bakery. A phantom monk has also been glimpsed here, walking past a window. Rumour has it there was a tunnel in the cellar which led to Blackfriars Monastery.

Among the more unusual haunted properties in Hereford is the modern Sainsbury's store. It was built on the site of a railway station. The ghostly elderly lady who has been seen wandering around the store and in the car park is thought to have been a passenger who lost her life at the station many years ago. The General Hospital has long since been converted into flats but is rumoured to still be haunted by a nurse who killed herself after an affair with a married doctor came to an end. She is a gentle soul, however, whose presence was known in the dead of night to comfort sleepless patients, who had no idea she was anything other than a caring, living woman.

The River Wye is haunted by a weeping woman in a rowing boat. Tradition has it that she is the grieving spirit of Isobel

The Old House in High Town, with the spire of St Peter's Church behind it. Both buildings are haunted. iStock

Chandos, daughter of the warden of Hereford Castle during the troubled reign of King Edward II. The king's favourite, Hugh le Despenser, came to the castle in disguise but fell in love with Isobel, and she with him. When the king's forces were poised to mount a surprise attack on the castle, Hugh urged Isobel to come away with him. She refused and warned her father instead. The defenders were therefore able to prepare in time and the attack failed. Hugh le Despenser's true identity was revealed and he was taken away and hanged. Isobel was so distraught at her unwitting betrayal and its consequences that she went slowly mad.

According to Roy Palmer, author of *Herefordshire Folklore*: 'She took to rowing alone on the Wye, and on one of her outings she drowned. Her ghost now rows down the same stretch of river, coming ashore where she used to meet Despenser. It weeps and wails, then returns the way it came, disappearing before it reaches the city. Ill fortune comes to any who see it.'

Hereford is also thought to number two more famous historical characters among its ghosts. Nell Gwyn, the orange seller turned actress who became the favourite of King Charles II's many mistresses, was originally from the city. She was born on Gwynne Street in the middle of the 17th century, although in those days it was called Pipe Lane. Her ambitious mother soon took the young Nell out of the provinces to London, and she grew into a woman of great charm and wit, beautiful enough to catch the eye of the monarch, and clever enough to keep him. Nell's ghost is said to be seen strolling down the street now named after her, dressed up in her finery, a saucy look in her eye.

Haunted Hereford author David Phelps has some doubts over the authenticity of Nell's ghost, wondering why she would haunt a place she'd not lived in except as a child. Gwynne Street is also haunted by a rather splendid Cavalier and, thanks to the connection with Nell Gwyn, this has been identified as Charles II himself. Mr Phelps is equally dubious about this identification, however, for so far as it is known the Merry Monarch never so much as visited Hereford. He considers both identifications to be wishful thinking. It's an appealing thought that these two glamorous figures from history might be haunting one little street in Hereford, but it is perhaps more likely that they are unconnected, two separate anonymous phantoms from a similar period.

Does Nell Gwyn haunt the street named after her, along with her lover Charles II?

THE HAUNTED TOWNS

King Charles II may or may not haunt Hereford but his ghost is also claimed for Ross-on-Wye. The Merry Monarch's face, with its distinctively prominent nose, has been seen peering out of an upstairs room in the hostelry named after him: the King Charles II Hotel in Broad Street. The phantom face was captured on film in 1973, but when a *Hereford Times* photographer tried to make a digital copy of the print thirty years later all sorts of strange things happened. According to Rupert Matthews (in his *Haunted Herefordshire*):

'No matter where he [photographer James Watkins] put the flash, it always reflected off the image of the ghost, ruining the copy. Then, in the one copy where the flash did not get in the way, an odd red blur obliterated the ghost instead.'

All very strange! Ross-on-Wye stands in the south-east of Herefordshire on the edge of the Forest of Dean. The tall spire of St Mary's, its parish church, is far and away the town's most prominent landmark and is visible for miles around. Ross-on-Wye has the distinction of being the place where British tourism was born. In 1782 an artist and antiquarian named William Gilpin published a book about his trip down the River Wye from Ross. His *Observations on the River Wye* was the UK's first illustrated guide book and inspired the love of 'picturesque' scenery which soon became a national obsession among the moneyed classes. Gilpin's book rapidly became a bestseller and was hugely influential. For a time Ross-on-Wye became one of the most visited towns in England. Other parts of the UK have since taken over as tourist attractions but this corner of the county remains an undeniably picturesque one and Ross is a charming old town.

One of the town's ghosts may possibly be the shade of one of its early tourists. However, she certainly doesn't seem to be enjoying herself. The ghost is described as being of an elderly woman sitting in an old-fashioned rowing boat on the Wye. She appears to be alone in the boat, her head bowed as if with sorrow, and she is not engaged in rowing; the boat drifts along with the current below the old stone bridge over the river. Did she originally have a companion, perhaps a son or husband, who lost his step in the boat and was drowned, leaving her to drift downstream in a state of shock?

The apparition bears a remarkable resemblance to the ghost of Isobel Chandos, which rows along the Wye at Hereford, weeping bitterly. It's likely that both ghosts represent a folk memory of some ancient, banshee-like spirit associated with the river.

Equally enigmatic is the spooky 'man in black' which lurks around the medieval King's Head pub in Ross's High Street. Even stranger are the 'stomping ghosts' which have been known to manifest in the High Street itself. There are three of them; they suddenly appear, stomp a few yards down the street and then just as abruptly vanish.

Elsewhere in the town is Copse Cross Street, where the Community Hospital is situated. Apparently, its original name was Corpse Cross Street because it was here that the body of a supposed suicide was buried. For centuries people who had taken their own lives were barred from being buried in consecrated ground. Instead they were frequently buried at crossroads in a custom dating back at least to Roman times. The man buried at Corpse Cross was Roger Mortimer, a gardener employed at a grand house called Alton Court just outside the town. He was a cheerful, comely fellow and a flirtation started up between him and the daughter of the house, Clara Markey. Clara was

Ross-on-Wye has a number of haunted locations, including the stretch of river running past it. iStock

unhappy because she was about to endure an arranged marriage with someone she didn't even like, let alone love. Her betrothed was wealthy, however, and that was all that mattered to Clara's hard-hearted father.

Unfortunately for Clara and Roger, their growing affection was observed and the girl's father was determined to make sure nothing would interfere with the advantageous match he had arranged. A few days before the marriage was due to take place Roger went missing from Alton Court. His body was found the following morning floating face down in the Wye where it flows beneath Wilton Bridge. A rapidly held inquest brought in a verdict of suicide, working on the assumption that Roger had been driven to despair by his hopeless infatuation with someone so much above his social station. Clara didn't believe this, however, and was distraught with not only grief but also a horrified suspicion as to her own father's involvement in Roger's death. Her father was merciless: there was to be no delay in the wedding.

As Mr Markey led his softly weeping daughter down the aisle of St Mary's Church, he was annoyed when she suddenly stopped dead. He turned to rebuke her and found she was staring at a space a few feet in front of her. Clara's face was a horror-stricken mask and it was clear she could see something no one else could. The bride-to-be uttered a bloodcurdling shriek and then fainted away into the arms of her cruel father, who had no choice but to cancel the wedding and take her home. No one found out what exactly Clara had seen in the church, for she never spoke again. The next day she went missing from Alton Court and was found wandering around Corpse Cross, apparently searching for Roger Mortimer's grave. Clara never recovered from the shock she had received in the church, nor the grief over the untimely and mysterious death of her lover. For the rest of her life she remained in a distracted state and every day she made the sad pilgrimage to Corpse Cross.

Even after her death, Clara continues to visit Copse Cross Street, as it is now known. Her apparition is described as an elderly downcast woman who leaves behind her a profound sense of depression. So familiar did the ghost become over the years that the route it takes from Alton Court to Copse Cross Street became known to townsfolk as Old Maid's Walk. It's possible that the mysterious ghost of the old woman on the Wye (see above) is also Clara, for the apparition is seen in approximately the place where Roger Mortimer's body was recovered.

The Iron Cross in Leominster was also a place of death. It was named after the gallows and gibbet which stood here centuries ago. In the early 17th century, during the reigns of Queen Elizabeth and James I, the Iron Cross became notorious for the execution of Catholics. At this time there were constant rumours of conspirators and terrorists seeking to overthrow the Protestant monarchy. Occasionally they were founded on fact, which only served to fuel suspicion towards Roman Catholics, especially those who came from abroad. At this paranoid time priests were outlawed and many innocent people were executed on suspicion of treason.

One of the latter unfortunates was Roger Cadwallader, a native of Stretton Sugwas, near Hereford. Roger travelled in Spain and Italy, studying his religion and becoming ordained as a priest. When he returned to England, he thought it wiser not to declare the fact that he was a now a priest, but he toured the Border Counties and those in the South-West, holding masses where and when required. This secrecy cost him his life, for he was arrested at Hereford in 1609, his behaviour being considered sufficiently suspicious to warrant his execution. He was hanged

St Mary's Church, Ross-on-Wye, where a bride-to-be witnessed a terrifying vision.
iStock

at the Iron Cross in Leominster the following year. He has since been beatified and is now properly known as Blessed Roger Cadwallader.

The venerable Talbot Hotel now stands on the crossroads, very close to where the gallows would have stood. It was built in the 1660s. For many years the hotel has been haunted by a tall, spectral figure, wrapped in a black cloak, his head hidden within a deep hood. Although the ghost is usually described as 'a monk', it is tempting to think that it is actually the martyred Blessed Roger Cadwallader.

One of the houses in South Street is haunted by a man of very different moral character to Roger Cadwallader. It is the ghost of a highwayman. It is seen descending a staircase and then vanishing through a wall where there was once a door.

There are two ghosts, one saintly, one sinful, in the historic market town of Leominster. iStock

Ghostly goings-on have been reported from a hotel in Hay-on-Wye, the bookshop capital of Britain. The poster called 'Jeff' who recounted his experiences at the hotel on the Castle of Spirits website decided it was better not to name it, so I am unable to identify it here. The owners told 'Jeff' of 'ghostly apparitions so lifelike' that guests had spoken to them before realising they were not of this world. They said the most haunted places in the hotel are the cellar and Room 11, where 'Jeff' elected to stay. Here he experienced an unnatural feeling of cold which seemed to move around the room. He also saw a kind of mist floating in a mass a few feet off the floor. This was accompanied by what he described as 'a distinctive scent … soapy like a faint perfume'.

Just outside the town, the Baskerville Hall Hotel has a haunted reputation, but one sufficiently different to distinguish it from the anonymous hotel described by 'Jeff'. According to the Haunted Rooms website, it has two ghosts. One is of a man and is seen on the main staircase, while the other is a White Lady who enjoys strolling round the rose garden. Tudor in style, the house actually dates from the 1830s. Arthur Conan Doyle stayed here on more than one occasion and, as we have seen, he may have been inspired by the story of Black Vaughan's ghostly black hound to write his novel *The Hound of the Baskervilles*.

The Falcon Hotel in Bromyard dates back to the reign of Henry VIII but its ghost apparently dates from a much more recent period. He is described as being 'a normal young man', dressed in the fashions of the 1950s or early 1960s. He hurries along an upstairs corridor, calling out 'Where is Anne?' before suddenly disappearing into thin air. Despite his unusually modern appearance, no one knows who he might have been, nor for that matter who Anne might have been, let alone why he is seeking her so urgently.

Another modern ghost manifested, just once, on 1 December 1950. On that day a woman was walking down Ledbury High Street when she spotted a friend, E.J.(Jack) Moeran, approaching her along the pavement. Moeran was a frequent visitor to Ledbury, where he would stay in the Rectory with his brother. Nevertheless, she was surprised to see him on this occasion because she had been told he'd gone to Ireland to stay with relatives. As Moeran passed, she tried to speak to him but he waved his hand at her in a familiar gesture meaning he didn't want to be disturbed. She took no offence at this. Moeran was a musician and he would often stroll around the town working out compositions in his head. His friends knew better than to distract him on such occasions.

A few days later, Jack Moeran's friends received upsetting news: he had died suddenly in Ireland. No one, of course, was more shocked than the woman who had passed him in Ledbury High Street that day. She later worked out that Moeran must have died at about the same time as she had seen him.

The medieval Market House in Ledbury's High Street. The apparition of someone dying or recently deceased was seen in the High Street in 1950. iStock

VILLAGE GHOSTS

We have visited a number of haunted pubs already. Others are to be found in Herefordshire's villages. Originally two properties, the upper storey of the Crown Inn, Lea, remains divided by a wall, each end converted into separate accommodation. One of these flats is the haunt of a ghostly woman in a long dress. She tends to appear in the room overlooking the street but has also been encountered on the stairs leading down to the bar. In common with the ghost of Clara Markey (see Ross-on-Wye in the previous chapter), this phantom female leaves behind her a feeling of depression, almost of dread.

In the restaurant area, an unexpected 'cover' sometimes intrudes. This is the ghost of an old man, sitting in a chair (also ghostly), quietly observing what's going on around him. Staff at the Crown have got used to leaving the space where he is wont to appear free of clutter. One year someone not in the know set up a Christmas tree there. After she had made the tree festive with tinsel and baubles, the proud staff member left the room. Moments later she heard a crash and found the Christmas tree upturned in the empty restaurant, the decorations scattered all over the floor.

A similar phenomenon is reported from the Lough Pool pub at Sellack. Here a chair is often found moved to a particular place in the restaurant, as if some returning spirit was recreating their favourite spot in the days when they were a regular. The scent of lavender lingers whenever this occurs, suggesting that the visitor from beyond is a woman.

We have already visited two churches in Herefordshire in which ghostly organ recitals are heard. The secular equivalent is the mysterious piano music, described by Rupert Matthews as 'a rather stately dance tune', which has been heard long after closing time in the Boot Inn, at Orleton. The tinkling ivories are accompanied by the equally inexplicable sounds of doors opening and closing and footsteps shuffling and clattering about the bar.

Strange noises also assailed the ancient Rhydspence Inn at Whitney-on-Wye. Centuries ago thieves murdered an old ferryman for the pot of pennies he had accumulated by taking people over to Hay and back. This pitiful haul cost the wretches their lives. They had committed their crime under the cover of darkness, so decided to stay at the Rhydspence for the rest of the night. They hid the pot of pennies in their room but were startled awake by a manic rattling sound. To their horror, they saw that the pot was shaking itself furiously. Nothing they tried would stop it from vibrating and making its unearthly din, and the rest of the guests were woken by it too. This was so clearly an intervention from beyond that the murderers soon broke down and confessed their crime. They were duly hanged.

The handsome, timber-framed New Inn in Pembridge has a name that is entirely inappropriate today, for it dates back to the early 14th century. It is considered the oldest New Inn in England, its name deriving from its conversion to a hostelry from its former function as firstly a farmhouse and then a courthouse.

Two apparitions have been reported from the New Inn, one upstairs and one downstairs. Upstairs there is the ghost of a beautiful but melancholy young woman in a long gown. She is believed to date from the period when the New Inn was still a farm. She was the farmer's daughter and therefore of some consequence in the local community. Her boyfriend felt himself unworthy of her suit, so he went abroad to seek his fortune, promising to return for her hand once he was a man of means.

But she never saw him again and the poor girl wasted away through longing and anxiety as to his fate. Her ghost only appears to women, perhaps in the hope of striking a chord of sisterly sympathy.

The ghost downstairs is of a young man in the red jacket typically worn by soldiers of a past century. He may have been a former customer of the inn or possibly the missing boyfriend of the lovelorn farmer's daughter upstairs. Perhaps he found soldiering the quickest way to earn some money but was killed in action before he could get word to his girl back home in Pembridge. If he has returned to the New Inn in search of her, it seems a cruel fate indeed that they remain separated by just one floor. A sad storey indeed!

The New Inn in Pembridge is actually more than 700 years old. Its two ghosts may be linked but they never meet. iStock

It's often no accident that in many villages the pub and the church are neighbours, for the church too was at the heart of village life for centuries, not only for worship, but for schooling, recreation (in the churchyard) and for general community interaction. There are a couple of haunted churches in Herefordshire.

The graveyard at St Weonards is haunted by arguably Herefordshire's weirdest spook – a pig with a saddle on its back. A monk-like figure also patrols the churchyard, and at one time it was said to be guarding a treasure hidden within the prominent mound beside the church. Legend had it that the mound contained St Weonard himself, buried within a solid gold coffin, but when it was excavated many years ago it was found to contain nothing more than a few bones and ashes.

The little church at Aconbury is now closed but may still be haunted by Sir Roger de Clifford, whose restless spirit troubled the village before being trapped in a bottle and then buried in the church wall. In the 19th century, Sir Roger's ghost began to appear again, in an especially macabre way. His hand was said to be seen emerging from the wall, reaching for members of the congregation. If it succeeded in touching an unlucky villager, that person was sure to die within the next twelve months.

Many villages have their own manor house as well as the church and pub, and a number of them are reputedly haunted. Pengethley Manor, for example, has two ghosts: a girl called Hetty who died in a fire in 1816 and a woman in a long black dress. The manor house is now a hotel. The grounds of Snodhill, the manor house belonging to Peterchurch, are haunted by a woman dressed all in white. When a member of the incumbent family at Snodhill is about to die, tradition has it a ghostly procession of a horse-drawn hearse, led by a priest and accompanied by torch-bearers, will be seen in the lane outside.

Eastnor Castle is situated just outside of the village of Eastnor. It is a splendid Gothic Revival house dating from the early 19th century and was built on an island to give it the appearance of having a moat. Tradition has it that the island was the burial place of a fabulous treasure, which has yet to be found, and that it is guarded by a huge supernatural raven. In 1998 a medium told the owners of Eastnor Castle that it was haunted by no fewer than thirteen ghosts, somewhat to their surprise. He then offered to rid the house of them, but they declined, never having been troubled by any of them.

Also a fortification in appearance only is Bollitree Castle at Weston under Penyard. In the 18th century local bigwig Thomas Hopkins ordered that it should be built in the medieval style to please his new wife (maybe she was an early goth), using stone from the ruined Penyard Castle. Unfortunately, the new Mrs Hopkins didn't particularly like the house or, as it turned out, Thomas either. Their marriage was not a happy one. The melancholy shade of Thomas Hopkins wanders about in Bollitree Castle's formal gardens, while his hard-to-please wife has been seen clumping up and down the staircase.

The genuinely medieval Hellens House at Much Marcle is said to be haunted by the unfortunate Hetty Walwyn, who ran away with an unsuitable man who then refused to marry her. Poor Hetty returned to Hellens House in a very sorry state, but she received no sympathy from her family. On the contrary, they locked her up in her bedroom for the rest of her life. The bars can still be seen on the windows of this room. Hetty must have been thoroughly miserable and her solitary confinement may well have unbalanced her mind. It's no wonder that she is rumoured to haunt the room. One possible sighting took place

Does Eastnor Castle really have thirteen ghosts? iStock

when a young guest slept here in the early 20th century. He woke to see someone in a dressing gown scurrying about the room, frantically but silently. The confined Hetty may well have paced her lifelong prison in the same desperate way.

Hellens House is also said to be haunted by a monk, murdered here during the Civil War, and by a nun-like figure. The latter can't be Hetty's ghost because it has been seen on the main staircase. It wears a long grey gown with a hood.

At Bryngwyn House, Much Dewchurch, two phantom figures have been seen struggling together in mortal combat. They are the echo of a remarkable incident which occurred in 1861, when a feud between Robert Pye and his neighbour Charles Bodenham erupted into violence. Bodenham was a Roman Catholic; Pye was a Protestant and a magistrate. When Pye tried to serve a summons on Bodenham for some spurious reason, they came to blows and Pye was killed in the fight.

One of Herefordshire's grandest show homes is the Georgian Berrington Hall, a National Trust property near Eye. Its ghost is comparatively modern, dating from the Second World War, when the hall was converted to be used as a hospital for wounded men. He strolls around the house, dressed in the uniform of an infantryman. Presumably he died here as a patient, for his ghost started being seen while the war was still being waged.

More unusual is the haunted railway station at Lyonshall. The station is no longer in use but this fact has apparently escaped the ghost of an elderly porter which is not infrequently seen here. He potters about, still wearing the uniform of yesteryear, as if seeking passengers to help.

A dangerous spook was trapped beneath Eardisland Bridge but its eerie presence can still be felt. iStock

This brief tour of Herefordshire's haunted villages comes to an end at one of its prettiest, Eardisland. The White Lady of Eardisland is an enigmatic figure which is seen strolling haughtily around the streets, but her identity is unknown. The nearby manor house is possessed of an even more mysterious entity simply described as a 'strange presence'. The handsome old bridge over the River Arrow, however, is the most haunted spot in the village. An invisible spook of enormous strength used to throw people, horses and even carriages over the parapet into the river, until it was 'prayed down' and laid under the bridge in a silver box. Nevertheless, people crossing the bridge after dark sometimes still report getting an eerie feeling and horses are notoriously shy of using it. Cars sometimes mysteriously break down when halfway over.

GHOSTS IN THE OPEN AIR

In addition to the ghosts of the towns and villages, a number are also known to haunt the woods and fields, the highways and byways, and creepy old ruins that have become exposed to the elements. The various manifestations of the Wild Hunt already discussed are good examples, of course.

The woods above Aconbury are said to be the haunt of a pair of young lovers united in death. Theirs is a tragic story. A farmer's daughter fell almost insanely in love with a young man from the village but became consumed with jealousy whenever she saw him speaking to any other girl. He was a popular youth and such conversations were bound to happen. The couple used to take walks in the woods overlooking the church, but as the months went by these tender meetings became marred by the girl's increasing jealousy and her baseless accusations. So convinced did she become that her boyfriend was seeing someone else behind her back that she went so far as to steal her father's shotgun and threaten him with it in order to get him to tell her 'the truth'. The gun went off; whether accidentally or otherwise won't ever be known. As the boy lay dying, his unbalanced girlfriend then took her own life in remorse. At least their ghosts seem to be happy, walking arm in arm through the woods just as they did before the green-eyed monster destroyed their lives.

In the middle of the 19th century, the good people of Pencombe decided to get rid of their old church and have a new one built instead. The old church was inconveniently situated some distance from the village and had steadily been falling into a state of neglect for many years. However, the congregation had reckoned without the feelings of their ancestors in the matter. The spectral forms of the long dead began to be seen hovering over their graves in the churchyard, and when this hint was not taken some of the ghosts took to processing down Church Lane towards the village. It was quickly decided to abandon plans to build a new church and instead the money raised was used to repair the old one. Those buried there were content, and returned to their comfortable graves.

At Kenchester a company of Roman soldiers has been seen on moonlit nights marching along the route of an old Roman road. They are presumed to be making their way to a small walled town called Magnis that has long since been obscured by grass and thicket. It seems the soldiers let no modern buildings get in their way, for one woman claimed she would see them marching straight through her cottage. Another householder whose home stood beside the Roman road said they often 'camped' in her garden.

During the Commonwealth, the regime run by Lord Protector Oliver Cromwell after the Civil War, a Dr Breton was established as minister of Pembridge. His wife's religious beliefs were not as Puritan as those of her husband and it always troubled her that he had been given land which had originally belonged to the church. After Dr Breton's death, his widow continued to receive the benefits of the property but she never felt easy in her heart about it. After her own death, her spirit appeared to her maidservant and compelled her to follow her to a field.

'Observe how much of this field I measure with my feet,' the ghost told the maid. 'All this belongs to the poor, it being gotten from them by unlawful means.'

The awestruck girl watched the ghost pace out the land and then went to find her former mistress's brother, who had inherited the property, to tell him what had happened. In future he ensured that any income from that parcel of land went to good works.

The brutal years of the Civil War have left a ghostly heritage throughout the British Isles. At Brampton Bryan in the north of Herefordshire can be found the ruins of a mighty medieval fortress. No less a figure than Oliver Cromwell himself is said to haunt the parkland round Brampton Bryan Castle. The castle was one of the few in Herefordshire whose owner had declared himself for Parliament rather than the King. This made it something of a target. While its owner, Sir Robert Harley, was away, Royalist forces besieged the castle knowing that it was now in the charge of his wife, the rather splendidly named Lady Brilliana. However, the lady proved tougher than expected and the castle held out against the siege for many months. Nevertheless, it was in a badly knocked-about shape by the time the war ended.

Sir Robert decided to abandon Brampton Bryan Castle and build a new house instead. Unfortunately, this didn't go to plan. On 3 September 1658, a terrific storm tore through Brampton Bryan, badly damaging the new mansion, which by this time was all but complete. On this date, and at about the time the storm struck, Oliver Cromwell died. Local people gossiped that the tempest was caused by the Lord Protector's angry soul raging through Sir Robert's property. Sir Robert was one of the noblemen who refused to sign the death warrant for Charles I. Cromwell's ghost was long afterwards said to be seen in the park at Brampton Bryan, a tall, imposing figure whom it is best to avoid. The phantom is generally seen in the autumn.

The ruined castle at Brampton Bryan. Oliver Cromwell's ghost is said to haunt the parkland around the ruin.

Goodrich Castle also suffered from a major siege during the Civil War. William Wordsworth called this castle 'the noblest ruin in Herefordshire' and few would disagree. The earliest fortress was built soon after the Norman Conquest and it was then greatly enlarged in the 12th century. During the Civil War Goodrich was keenly fought over and was in both Parliamentarian and Royalist hands at different times. While held by the Royalists, it was besieged by Colonel John Birch, who had far more powerful artillery at his disposal than those who laid siege to Brampton Bryan. His weapons included a massive mortar nicknamed 'Roaring Meg', which can still be seen at Goodrich Castle (the ruin is in the care of English Heritage). The Royalists simply couldn't withstand such a barrage and were forced to capitulate.

Colonel Birch had a personal as well as a professional interest in forcing the surrender of the Royalist garrison. His niece, Alice, had eloped with a cavalry officer named Sir Charles Clifford, and he was known to be stationed at Goodrich Castle, his young bride by his side. Birch had sworn vengeance on Sir Charles, who knew he could expect no mercy once the walls were breached. His commanding officer arranged to cause a diversion in the hope that Sir Charles could sneak out and ride away under cover of darkness while the besiegers were distracted. Unfortunately, desperate not to be parted from her husband, Alice Birch insisted on accompanying him. She slowed him down and as they were trying to ford the river, they were spotted. Riflemen opened fire and the young couple fell to their deaths in the swirling waters.

This tragedy is said to still be played out in ghostly form. A horse is seen to ride pell-mell to the river's bank, a young woman clutching the waist of the Cavalier urging it on. Suddenly the horse rears and the riders are thrown down. Then the vision vanishes. Sir Charles and Alice have also been seen wandering through the ruins and in the fields around it. They saunter arm in arm, as if still enjoying the brief period of peace afforded them before the arrival of the vengeful Colonel Birch and his engines of war.

At Colwall, the area around the local manor house, Barton Court, is haunted by Lady Tempest. This unlucky young woman was wooed in an unusual manner by her future husband, the unscrupulous Sir Henry Tempest, who was desperate for money.

To win the hand of Sarah Lambert, a naïve young heiress, he disguised himself as an old gypsy woman and convinced her to visit the village church the following day at a certain time, telling her that there she would meet the man she was destined to marry. Of course, this man was the crafty Sir Henry, who made sure he was at the church when Sarah, full of curiosity, called in at the appointed time.

Sarah did not recognise Sir Henry as the gypsy fortune teller and he used all of his charm to fascinate her. Her father smelled a rat and was not so keen on Sir Henry's suit, however. The impoverished baronet convinced Sarah to elope with him and, in the pouring rain one night she went to meet his carriage. Sir Henry couldn't be bothered going out himself on such a night, even to whisk away his doting heiress, and his coachman got the rendezvous wrong. Poor Sarah wandered around in the rain, getting soaked through, until at last Sir Henry's coachman found her in a pitiable state in a lane called Barton Holloway.

Even this misadventure did not bring an end to Sarah's affections and she married her uncouth baronet. The triumphant Sir Henry took the newly entitled Lady Tempest back to her home, Hope End House, and lost no time in booting out her dismayed father, who went to live in Barton Court instead. It wasn't long before Sir Henry served his bride in the same way and Sarah soon found herself cast out, too. The distraught woman made her way to Barton Court but her father refused to let her in, his wounded pride making him deaf to her tearful entreaties. Sarah was eventually taken in by a less hard-hearted relative but she died a broken and disappointed woman.

After Lady Tempest's death, her ghost took to haunting the grounds of Barton Court, as if still trying to gain admittance to the house from which she was so cruelly turned away. In the 19th century, the young men of the house apparently used to take pot shots at the ghost. Sarah also haunted a bridge over Barton Holloway, the place where she had wandered in her misery waiting for Sir Henry's coach.

Gravenor's Bridge, near Middleton on the Hill, is also haunted by a similarly unhappy woman. Dressed all in white, she can be seen standing on the bridge when the moon is bright. She may be the spirit of a young woman who drowned herself here after being jilted on her wedding day. Another phantom female, this time dressed in grey and wearing a long cloak, has startled motorists by standing in the middle of a minor road near Hentland, just round a bend. She vanishes before there is any collision. A ghostly woman has been seen riding a grey horse near Yarpole, oblivious to any traffic.

An alarming phenomenon has been reported on the road leading past Stoke Lacy church, on towards Bromyard. Some drivers have reported the terrifying experience of feeling invisible hands grab their steering wheel as if someone is trying to prevent them safely making the upcoming bend in the road. It has been suggested that a tragic event echoing this experience took place in the 1930s when bystanders watched as a car hurtled past, the man at the wheel and the woman by his side having a blazing row. The woman was seen to grab the steering wheel and apparently forced the car to smash into a wall with fatal consequences.

Finally, there is the case of a *haunting*, rather than a *haunted*, house at Callow Hill, near Hereford. In the early 19th century Callow Farm was a coaching inn. It had an evil reputation as a meeting place for footpads and highwaymen, and guests who stayed overnight were all too frequently never seen again. Suspicions aroused, the inn was finally raided by the authorities and they learnt that many guests had been robbed and murdered, their bodies afterwards being carried to a house two fields away, where they were buried in the cellar. For years afterwards the shades of crouched men carrying heavy burdens between them were observed creeping across the fields, and the house became shunned. Eventually, it was pulled down as an affront to the neighbourhood. Nevertheless the house is still sometimes to be seen, in phantom form, standing in its old situation on Callow Hill.

*The mighty ruins of Goodrich Castle, where the doomed Sir Charles Clifford and
his bride have been seen in ghostly form. iStock*